ESTHER, FROG QUEEN

Julie Marie Myatt

BROADWAY PLAY PUBLISHING INC
New York
www.broadwayplaypublishing.com
info@broadwayplaypublishing.com

Cover image: Julie Marie Myatt

First edition: September 2022
I S B N: 978-0-88145-945-6

Book design: Marie Donovan
Page make-up: Adobe InDesign
Typeface: Palatino

ESTHER, FROG QUEEN was commissioned by Yale Repertory Theatre.

CHARACTERS & SETTING

MARTIN
GINA, *voice O S*
ESTHER
GERALD
RUTH
LILY

Time: Present
Place: Amphibian Lab

NOTE ON MUSIC

For performance of copyrighted songs, arrangements
or recordings referenced in this play, permission
of the copyright owner(s) must be obtained. Other
songs, arrangements or recordings may be substituted
provided permission from the copyright owner(s) of
such songs, arrangements or recordings is obtained,
or songs, arrangements or recordings in the public
domain may be substituted.

"What's at stake here is a liveable world."
Robert Watson, Chairman of The Intergovernmental
Science-Policy Platform on Biodiversity and Ecosystem
Services

Prologue

(Darkness)

(Music)

(The sound of rainforest frogs)

(A woman laughing with friends.)

(A party?)

(More laughing and singing joins in.)

(The sound of footsteps on branches. A clearing of the throat.)

(The sound of the frogs abruptly stops.)

(The music stops. A bright light searches.)

(ESTHER is caught in this bright light. She's surrounded.)

Scene 1

(Lights up on MARTIN. He waits on a chair, in new green suit. He's clearly not comfortable. It's too formal for him, but he's trying. A chair sits empty beside him.)

(He is surrounded by odd objects to make him feel this is his home. A small piano and guitar is thrown in there as well as fake plants and fake logs, a small fake pond [That looks much like a plastic baby pool].)

(MARTIN adjusts his tie. Impatient)

(MARTIN looks around. Tries to relax. Stares into space.)

MARTIN: What's she look like?

(Silence)

MARTIN: Am I not allowed to ask that?

VOICE: *(O S)* No.

MARTIN: She's unattractive.

VOICE: *(O S)* I didn't say that.

MARTIN: What's wrong with her?

VOICE: *(O S)* Nothing.

MARTIN: Is she pretty? It's a simple question.

VOICE: *(O S)* Relax.

MARTIN: So she's not pretty.

VOICE: *(O S)* Martin.

MARTIN: Is she nice?

VOICE: *(O S)* Don't worry.

MARTIN: Smart?

VOICE: *(O S)* Please.

MARTIN: She's not nice? And she's dumb?

VOICE: *(O S)* I didn't say that.

MARTIN: There's a lot you seem to not be saying.

VOICE: *(O S)* It's just not relevant.

MARTIN: To me it is.

VOICE: *(O S)* It doesn't matter.

MARTIN: It matters to me.

VOICE: *(O S)* We have bigger goals here.

MARTIN: Speak for yourself.

(Big sigh O S)

VOICE: *(O S)* She's perfect.

MARTIN: Really?

VOICE: *(O S)* Absolutely. A ten.

MARTIN: Wow.

(Silence)

MARTIN: Are you saying she's too good for me?

VOICE: *(O S)* No.

MARTIN: A ten....

(Silence)

MARTIN: What am I?

VOICE: *(O S)* A six.

MARTIN: Six?

VOICE: *(O S)* That's as high as men get.

(MARTIN smells his breath.)

MARTIN: Is bad breath good or bad?

VOICE: *(O S)* Bad.

(MARTIN smells it again.)

MARTIN: Are you sure?

VOICE: *(O S)* Yes.

(MARTIN fixes his collar. It's very stiff.)

MARTIN: A ten... No. I can't do it. This is too stressful. Let's call it off.

VOICE: *(O S)* It's too late.

MARTIN: What if she doesn't like me?

VOICE: *(O S)* That's impossible.

MARTIN: I'm a six.

VOICE: *(O S)* Women can turn a six into a eight with a little imagination. Trust me.

MARTIN: But I have a good life. It's not a great life. It's not an exciting life. It's in no way a meaningful life. It's sad and limited and much too quiet, but it's mine.

Like a wart. I'm used to it. I've gotten used to it. Why change now?

VOICE: *(O S)* Stop.

MARTIN: I've made peace with myself. Played by myself. With myself.

VOICE: *(O S)* Martin.

MARTIN: What?

VOICE: *(O S)* Please.

MARTIN: What?

VOICE: *(O S)* Maybe talk less when she arrives.

MARTIN: Why?

VOICE: *(O S)* Just let her do the talking.

MARTIN: Why? Is there something weird about my voice?

VOICE: *(O S)* No.

MARTIN: Do you think it's irritating?

VOICE: *(O S)* No.

MARTIN: How am I supposed to measure the sound of my own voice or know if it's extremely annoying, grating, or off-putting?

VOICE: *(O S)* It's not.

MARTIN: Then why did you say that?

VOICE: *(O S)* I would hate for you to say something you regret.

MARTIN: Like what?

VOICE: *(O S)* Like…you play with yourself.

MARTIN: But I do.

VOICE: *(O S)* Okay.

MARTIN: You want me to pretend to be someone I'm not?

VOICE: *(O S)* No.

MARTIN: Is this how this is going to go? You want me to ACT like someone else? Just so she'll like me?

VOICE: *(O S)* Of course not.

MARTIN: What did you tell her about me?

VOICE: *(O S)* Nothing.

MARTIN: Then why did you say that?

VOICE: *(O S)* I don't know. I'm nervous.

MARTIN: This was your idea.

VOICE: *(O S)* It wasn't just mine.

MARTIN: Really?

VOICE: *(O S)* And you'll be happy about it. I promise.

MARTIN: I didn't ask for any of this. I was content.

VOICE: *(O S)* We both know that's not true.

MARTIN: I was. *(He picks his teeth.)*

VOICE: *(O S)* Don't do that.

MARTIN: What?

VOICE: *(O S)* Pick your teeth.

MARTIN: How am I supposed to get the food out?

VOICE: *(O S)* I don't know, but—

MARTIN: You are really doing a number on my confidence.

VOICE: *(O S)* I'm sorry.

MARTIN: Next thing you're going to tell me is that I can't fart.

VOICE: *(O S)* You can't.

MARTIN: What?

VOICE: *(O S)* No.

MARTIN: That's not healthy.

VOICE: *(O S)* Who told you that?

MARTIN: My father. They were his last words to me.

VOICE: *(O S)* Not true.

MARTIN: Have you seen my diet?

VOICE: *(O S)* Hold it in. You want to make a good impression.

MARTIN: I'm a six!

VOICE: *(O S)* Still.

MARTIN: Who does she think she's meeting? Prince Charming?

VOICE: *(O S)* I forget you've never done this before.

MARTIN: No! I haven't! And you're making me very very nervous.

VOICE: *(O S)* I'm sorry. I just want it to work out. This is for you. Both of you.

MARTIN: Then please let Me. Be. Me.

VOICE: *(O S)* I'll try.

MARTIN: This suit is so uncomfortable. I feel ridiculous.

VOICE: *(O S)* I like it.

MARTIN: Where did you get it?

VOICE: *(O S)* I made it.

MARTIN: Out of what? It's stiff.

VOICE: *(O S)* Felt.

MARTIN: I don't know what that is.

VOICE: *(O S)* It's just an inexpensive material.

MARTIN: You gave me a cheap suit? Now she'll think I'm cheap and stingy with money. Or a grifter.

VOICE: *(O S)* It took me hours to sew it, by hand—

MARTIN: I feel silly. *(He stands. One of his legs is shorter than the other. He looks at himself.)* Do you find my body unbecoming?

(Silence)

VOICE: *(O S)* No.

MARTIN: That was a long pause.

VOICE: *(O S)* I don't.

MARTIN: Then why am I wearing it?

VOICE: *(O S)* It makes me laugh.

MARTIN: I'm taking it off.

VOICE: *(O S)* No, no, no. You look great. Oh shit. Here she comes. Here she comes. Suck in your stomach.

MARTIN: What?

(ESTHER is pushed in to the room with a big shove. She has the look of someone who has just been ripped from her home, and placed in this now very weird, small, sterile room.)

(But, she is undeniably, regal.)

VOICE: *(O S)* The moment we've all been waiting for! *(Like a royal bugle)* Dan ta da daaaa!

(ESTHER just stares at MARTIN.)

VOICE: *(O S)* Sheila. Martin. Martin. Sheila. Martin. Sheila, Sheila Martin.

(MARTIN bows. His pants rip.)

MARTIN: Damn it.

VOICE: *(O S)* It's nothing. It's fine.

MARTIN: It's not fine. Look?

VOICE: *(O S)* Leave it.

MARTIN: But there's a draft—

VOICE: *(O S)* Leave it! Oh my. What a moment. Now, I know this may feel awkward at first, for both of you, but things take time. *(Nervous laugh)* I don't believe in love at first sight. Not anymore. I did when I was young of course, but, but enough about me. I'm going to give you two some privacy to get to know each other.

MARTIN: Privacy?

VOICE: *(O S)* I'm sure you all have a lot to talk about.

MARTIN: What privacy? I can see you looking at me out there.

VOICE: *(O S)* No you can't.

MARTIN: I see your eyes. Right now.

VOICE: *(O S)* Martin.

(The sound of a mic rustling.)

MARTIN: She's still watching us. Someone's always watching. It's very post-modern. It does a number on your self-confidence. *(Silence)* I'm sure that's why I overeat. *(Silence)* Maybe that's not the Only reason I overeat. If I'm honest with myself. There's boredom. Anxiety.

(ESTHER's looking for exits.)

MARTIN: Mother issues. *(Silence)* Despair. *(Silence)* A general unrest. *(Silence)* Fear.

ESTHER: How long have you been here?

MARTIN: Ten years, more or less. I don't have a clock, so…

(ESTHER is starting to panic.)

MARTIN: I heard you were hard to find. You made the news. We made the news. Gina was all giddy about it. Like she was famous. *(Silence)* What's it like? Out there. In the wild. *(Silence)* Do you have to catch your own food out there? I wouldn't like that. *(Silence)* All that running and chasing. And waiting. Planning. *(Silence)* And then of course being eaten before you even have a chance to have dinner yourself. That's no way to end the day. *(Silence)* Like Pinnoccio in the belly of the whale. But dead. *(Silence)* I like your hair. *(Silence)* It's kind of all over the place. Kind of wind-swept. Sexy. *(Silence)* I'm feeling all kinds of feelings I've never felt before. *(Silence)* Gina said you were a ten, and I agree. Then again, I've never seen any other number. *(He moves closer to her.)* Do all ten's have lips like that? And eyes? *(Silence)* Can I touch your face?

ESTHER: No.

MARTIN: Please? It looks soft.

ESTHER: No.

(ESTHER moves away from MARTIN.)

MARTIN: I like your vibe. Kind of edgy. Sexy and rough. And I'm getting a kind of smell…what is that, anger? Panic? Urine?

ESTHER: Do you have any idea what I just went through?

MARTIN: Can I sing you a song?

ESTHER: No.

MARTIN: It helps me relax. *(He goes over to his piano.)* I'm very good. You'll see. *(Singing)*
Oh Sheila Sheila Sheila, where you been all my life?
Now before we go any further, I'll cut to the chase,
bend on one knee, ask for your hand….
Will you be my wife?
(He's not very good. Singing)
Oh Sheila, Sheila, Sheila, all the fun we'll share
It's you and me forever, making lots of babies,
swimmin, livin', dreamin, without a care
Sheila, Sheila—

ESTHER: My name is Esther Kaslaandovenaianovamos.

MARTIN: What?

ESTHER: My name is Esther.

MARTIN: *(Singing)*
First I hear your name was Sheila, then I hear it's not.
You tell me to call you Esther
Kaslamalangadingdong—

ESTHER: Uh—

MARTIN: *(Singing)*
I think, well, shit, that's a lot
Maybe I'll just call you honey, or sweetie, or sugar, or
baby—

ESTHER: Whatever you have in mind, it's not going to
happen.

MARTIN: *(Singing)*
You don't even know me, I'm pretty great.

ESTHER: I'll die if I stay here.

MARTIN: You won't die. Look at me. *(Singing)*
"Look at me, I'm Sandra Dee."

ESTHER: You're what I'm afraid of.

MARTIN: *(Singing)*
That's not very nice.

ESTHER: Please.

MARTIN: *(Singing)*
I am very sensitive and insecure and prone to long
bouts of depression—

ESTHER: Please stop.

VOICE: *(O S)* Enough with the singing, Martin.

(MARTIN *stops.)*

MARTIN: I suppose I don't want overwhelm you with all of my talent in one go. *(He stands and tries to cover up his split pants.)* Did they give you that outfit?

ESTHER: Outfit?

MARTIN: Your clothes.

ESTHER: Why would they give me clothes?

MARTIN: For me.

ESTHER: Why?

MARTIN: To dress you up. For me.

ESTHER: To what end?

MARTIN: To impress me....?

ESTHER: What year is this? Am I stuck in a time machine?

MARTIN: I don't have a clock. I told you.

(ESTHER looks MARTIN over.)

ESTHER: Is that for me?

MARTIN: Yes. They made it. She made it. Gina.

ESTHER: How does she understand us? How do we hear her?

MARTIN: She's in control.

ESTHER: How?

MARTIN: Just the way it is. *(He tries to straighten himself up.)* This is kind of a big deal, you know. You and me. I don't know if you are aware. Many are invested in me. And now, I'm not alone anymore. *(He smiles.)* I can be a father. You can save us.

ESTHER: Us?

MARTIN: Didn't they tell you?

ESTHER: I'm not having kids.

MARTIN: There's only two of us left.

ESTHER: So.

MARTIN: It's our duty.

ESTHER: I don't want them.

MARTIN: But you have to.

ESTHER: I don't want them.

MARTIN: What about our future?

ESTHER: *Our?* With that breath?

MARTIN: *(Hiding his mouth)* Yes.

ESTHER: A life like this? No.

MARTIN: It's not that bad.

ESTHER: No. I'm going home.

MARTIN: You won't get out of here. Look around.

ESTHER: We'll see.

MARTIN: I tried it once. When I was young. That's why my leg is like it is.

ESTHER: Did they punish you?

MARTIN: No I got stuck. It wasn't pretty. It was bent all this way and that.

ESTHER: They wouldn't just let you go?

MARTIN: With a bad leg? That's inhumane. I'd be gobbled alive. So, I say, Esther Ka…whatever…now that you're here, we might as well do what's best for everyone and have some babies, save the species, put that mortgage down on the three bedroom ranch, and, maybe, maybe even have a little fun in between. *(He winks.)* I'm not well-versed in the romance area, but I've been told that we just need get to know each other a little better, to move this party forward in the right sexual direction. Can I touch you?

ESTHER: No.

MARTIN: Okay. *(He takes out a note pad.)* Interests?

ESTHER: What?

MARTIN: What are your interests? Your hobbies? Hopes and Dreams? Bucket list? Personally, I make maps. Write and play music and sing, as you are now aware. Sometimes I dance, when the mood strikes me. I have a well-rounded life to offer you. What have you got for me?

(ESTHER just looks at MARTIN.)

MARTIN: What do you bring to the table?

ESTHER: What table?

MARTIN: Our relationship. Future family.

VOICE: *(O S)* How's it going in there?

MARTIN: She hates the suit. And she think she's going home.

VOICE: *(O S)* It's adorable. And no.

MARTIN: Oh, and her name is Esther.

VOICE: *(O S)* Esther? Too Biblical. We like the name Sheila. We're going with Sheila. This is science. Please.

ESTHER: Take me home.

VOICE: *(O S)* You are home.

ESTHER: Please lady. I'm begging you. Please. Woman to woman.

VOICE: *(O S)* What does gender have to do with it?

ESTHER: Please. Help me. This isn't for me. Let me go.

VOICE: *(O S)* Why don't you and Martin get to know each other a little better, and then see how you feel.

ESTHER: I'm begging you.

VOICE: *(O S)* Martin has been anticipating this day for a long time.

MARTIN: Not really. I'd given up.

VOICE: *(O S)* Martin.

ESTHER: I will get on my hands and knees. Please. Don't make me stay here. Please. I'll die. *(She gets on her hands and knees.)*Please let me go home. Please.

VOICE: *(O S)* Martin, help her up.

MARTIN: What?

VOICE: *(O S)* Help her up.

MARTIN: How?

VOICE: *(O S)* Just...

(MARTIN reaches for ESTHER.)

ESTHER: Don't—

MARTIN: But I'm trying—

ESTHER: Don't!

MARTIN: I'm not good at this.

ESTHER: You stink.

MARTIN: You don't smell all that great either, but I didn't want to say anything.

VOICE: *(O S)* Let's not pick at each other.

MARTIN: She started it.

VOICE: *(O S)* Martin.

MARTIN: She did!

(Big sigh O S)

VOICE: *(O S)* I think if you two relax, sit down and talk awhile, you will find you actually have a lot in common. Martin, why don't you ask Sheila about her life and go from there.

ESTHER: Let me go.

MARTIN: She's judgmental. I can tell.

VOICE: *(O S)* See what's underneath the judgement.
Insecurity maybe?

ESTHER: LET ME GO!

MARTIN: What am I supposed to say? She's hysterical.

ESTHER: LET ME GO!

VOICE: *(O S)* Say "Tell me about yourself."

MARTIN: Then what?

ESTHER: LET ME GO!

VOICE: *(O S)* Just keep asking her about her. And nod
and listen and nod some more.

ESTHER: LET ME GO!

VOICE: *(O S)* But don't just ask one question and then
jump back to talk about yourself. And then ramble on
and on. My husband does that and I hate it.

ESTHER: LET ME GO!

MARTIN: What if she won't answer?

ESTHER: LET ME GO!

VOICE: *(O S)* Be creative.

MARTIN: This is very stressful.

ESTHER: LET ME GO!

VOICE: *(O S)* I'm not going to let you go so you can go
ahead and stop screaming at me.

ESTHER: Fuck you.

VOICE: *(O S)* Insults aren't useful either.

(ESTHER kicks over the chairs.)

VOICE: *(O S)* Or outbursts.

MARTIN: I'm not sure I'm cut out for women.

VOICE: *(O S)* I'll leave you two alone.

ESTHER: Leave us really alone.

VOICE: *(O S)* That's what I just said—

ESTHER: No. I want real privacy.

VOICE: *(O S)* I told you I was going to—

ESTHER: I'll kill him if you don't give us some real privacy.

MARTIN: Kill me?

ESTHER: I mean it, Lady.

VOICE: *(O S)* My name is Gina.

ESTHER: I like Lady. I'm going with Lady.

VOICE: *(O S)* I have a PhD.

ESTHER: It won't stop me from killing him if you don't leave us alone. Really alone.

MARTIN: Don't do it.

VOICE: *(O S)* It is my job to observe you.

ESTHER: I don't want to see your blinking eyes out there. *(Silence)* Step away. Now. *(Silence)* Now.

VOICE: *(O S)* I'm trusting you, Sheila.

MARTIN: I'm not. You're going to leave me alone with her?

VOICE: *(O S)* Man up, Martin.

MARTIN: What's that supposed to mean?

VOICE: *(O S)* Stop being weird and making this all about you. You'll ruin everything.

MARTIN: But it is about me.

VOICE: *(O S)* Fake it.

(The sound of the mic O S)

MARTIN: Please. Esther Ka whatchamacall it. You may think that all this doesn't look like much, but it's still my life, and I've gotten used to it. I want to live.

ESTHER: I'm not going to kill you.

MARTIN: You sure?

ESTHER: Yet.

MARTIN: You're making me anxious. I'm hungry.

ESTHER: I have a feeling you came that way.

MARTIN: I had a traumatic childhood.

ESTHER: We all did. *(She looks for an exit.)*

MARTIN: Really? *(Silence)* Did you have brothers and sisters?

ESTHER: Of course. *(She continues looking.)* You didn't have siblings?

MARTIN: I try not to think about them.

ESTHER: Do you miss them?

MARTIN: Gina says I'm not supposed to talk about me.

ESTHER: It's a simple question. Do you miss them?

(ESTHER stops, looks at MARTIN.)

(MARTIN gets emotional. Surprising himself.)

MARTIN: Yes. *(He tries to recover.)* I'm sorry.

ESTHER: What for?

MARTIN: We barely know each other.

ESTHER: So you can't cry?

(MARTIN shrugs.)

ESTHER: I'd cry my eyes out if this was my life.

(MARTIN is trying to keep it together.)

MARTIN: I have my hobbies. My music.

ESTHER: Music isn't freedom.

MARTIN: Freedom of the spirit.

ESTHER: Or family. *(She returns to her search.)*

MARTIN: You don't have family.

ESTHER: I have friends.

MARTIN: It's not the same.

ESTHER: Friends can be even better than family.

MARTIN: I've never heard that.

ESTHER: There's a lot you don't know.

MARTIN: Well, that's why they found me you. You're my family now. *(Silence)* Right?

(A rustle off-stage on the mic. A clearing of the throat)

(ESTHER looks.)

ESTHER: *(Yelling)* I'LL EAT THIS SON OF A BITCH RIGHT NOW IF YOU DON'T STEP AWAY, LADY!

MARTIN: Eat me?

ESTHER: I don't like her.

MARTIN: Why would you eat me?

ESTHER: Relax.

MARTIN: You're making it very hard.

ESTHER: And I wouldn't eat you. I'd tear you to pieces. Or maybe just smash your head in with one of those fake logs.

MARTIN: Jesus.

(ESTHER laughs.)

MARTIN: You aren't what I expected.

ESTHER: You think they'd throw me in here and I'd take one look at you, gasp, smile, swoon, giggle, throw back my hair, and bend over and let you fuck me?

MARTIN: Kinda.

ESTHER: You have been brainwashed.

MARTIN: I believe in love.

ESTHER: That's not love.

MARTIN: A version.

ESTHER: Scientists are hopeless romantics.

MARTIN: Gina likes science fiction.

ESTHER: Figures.

MARTIN: I read a lot of Kant. Kafka. Derrida.

ESTHER: Why?

MARTIN: Helps me sleep.

ESTHER: Do you remember at all what it's like out there?

MARTIN: Where?

ESTHER: Where you belong? *(Silence)* In the forest?

MARTIN: I belong here now.

ESTHER: Trapped inside a glass world, that is trapped inside some dusty old heterosexual dream?

MARTIN: I don't know that I'd call this a dream—

ESTHER: And now they're trying to shove me into it with you, just so that I too can live out their backward middle-class fantasies of success and happiness.

MARTIN: I think they're just trying to save the species.

ESTHER: Same thing.

MARTIN: I don't think so.

ESTHER: What are they saving us for? Who?

MARTIN: For us. Everyone. The world.

ESTHER: You believe that?

MARTIN: I think so.

ESTHER: Why would they do that?

MARTIN: The future needs frogs. We eat things.

ESTHER: If we can find it.

MARTIN: Every bit counts. "We all have to do our part!"

ESTHER: Have you been out there?

MARTIN: I think we've made that pretty clear—

ESTHER: Disease has wiped us all out. There's no where to live.

MARTIN: Why do you want to go back?

ESTHER: It's home. I love it.

MARTIN: I hear it's hot.

ESTHER: But, if they think for one second I'd subject a kid to any of it, or *this, this nightmare,* just for the sake of our species survival in this bleak future, they are seriously mistaken.

MARTIN: *This* is decent housing. Free food. Good health. Security.

ESTHER: Look around you.

MARTIN: It could use some dusting, I know, but—

ESTHER: YOU LIVE IN A GLASS CAGE AND YOU DON'T KNOW IT!

MARTIN: I GET SIX MEALS A DAY AND HAVE PLENTY OF SPACE TO SWIM AND COMPOSE MY MUSIC!

ESTHER: THAT'S NOT LIVING!

MARTIN: NO ONE IS CHASING ME!

ESTHER: YOU COULD USE THE EXERCISE!

MARTIN: I'M DISEASE-FREE!

ESTHER: YOUR MIND ISN'T!

(MARTIN *is out of breath.*)

MARTIN: I'm not used to so much yelling.

ESTHER: This isn't living, Martin.

MARTIN: It feels like living to me. And it's safe.

ESTHER: IN A GLASS FUCKING CAGE!?!

MARTIN: You'd rather live out there, in fear? Always watching your back? Alone?

ESTHER: Me, yes.

MARTIN: YOU'RE VERY CONFUSING!

ESTHER: YOU'RE VERY STUPID!

VOICE: *(O S)* Is there a problem in there?

MARTIN: She hates me.

ESTHER: I don't hate you.

MARTIN: You don't like me.

ESTHER: I don't want to have sex with you or live with you or touch you or hear your Stepford thoughts or have anything to do with this whole backward ecological experiment.

*(*MARTIN *does the math in his head.)*

MARTIN: That's not hate?

ESTHER: No.

MARTIN: What is it?

ESTHER: Insight.

MARTIN: She's a lesbian. You found me a lesbian.

VOICE: *(O S)* Impossible.

ESTHER: I'm not a lesbian. But it's not impossible.

MARTIN: I just repulse you?

ESTHER: Yes.

MARTIN: Take her back, Gina.

ESTHER: It's not just you, it's what you want from me. The whole package.

MARTIN: I'm normal. I want children! I don't want to die with nothing.

ESTHER: BE MORE CREATIVE, FOR GOD'S SAKE! Is that the answer to everything? Have children? Reproduce? Then what, huh? What are *they* left with? Who will take care of *them*?

VOICE: *(O S)* Calm down.

ESTHER: No one ever thinks of that.

VOICE: *(O S)* We've thought of everything, Sheila.

ESTHER: I doubt that. I told you to give us privacy—

VOICE: *(O S)* Now maybe you won't be extinct.

ESTHER: That's our fate. Let us have it.

VOICE: *(O S)* That's very selfish. If we want to be of use, Sheila, to any species, we must have children. Give of ourselves. Give them the best of everything. Give them everything they need to thrive and find the life they want. What would we do without frogs?

ESTHER: Not everyone can afford the best, by the way.

VOICE: *(O S)* Of course they can. If they try hard enough. We all have to strive for something better. Make sacrifices to give children what they need and want. You have to make sacrifices too, Sheila.

ESTHER: That's an excuse to create the world *you* want. It has nothing to do with them. Talk about selfish.

MARTIN: I thought kids were about fun and survival.

ESTHER: You really have zero imagination.

MARTIN: YOU DON'T EVEN KNOW ME!

ESTHER: I WOULD NEVER HAVE SEX WITH AN IDIOT!

VOICE: *(O S)* Okay, okay. Let's just all calm down. We've all gotten off to a shaky start. *(Big sigh)* What can

I do to make this all better? Anyone hungry? I think
you're both just hungry.

MARTIN: I can't live with her. She yells too much.

VOICE: *(O S)* Martin.

MARTIN: She hates everything, including children.
She's psychotic.

ESTHER: I don't hate children.

MARTIN: Probably hates puppies too. And rainbows.

VOICE: *(O S)* She's never held a baby. It's magical.
When a woman gives up on the dream of motherhood,
this is what happens.

ESTHER: Uh huh.

MARTIN: She judges everything I say.

ESTHER: You say stupid things. *(She nonchalantly looks
through* MARTIN's *stack of maps.)*

VOICE: *(O S)* You're talking about yourself too much.

MARTIN: Who else am I supposed to talk about?!

VOICE: *(O S)* Martin.

MARTIN: She made me. And she made me cry.

VOICE: *(O S)* Well, that's not hard.

MARTIN: Asking about my childhood. Who does that?

VOICE: *(O S)* Oh dear. We don't like to talk about that.

MARTIN: All your stupid effort in the forest, digging
and digging in dirt and searching for years, and you
find me a psychopath?

VOICE: *(O S)* Why don't I send in a nice tray of
delicious food. That will make everyone feel better.

MARTIN: I want extra dessert. A pie. No, a cake. Make
it a cake. A big one.

VOICE: *(O S)* Martin, we've talked about this.

MARTIN: Five layers. Extra frosting.

VOICE: *(O S)* You're stress eating.

MARTIN: This is stressful. I need some cake!

VOICE: *(O S)* Okay. Fine. We'll bring in some cake. What else? Music?

MARTIN: None of your music. Please. It gives me a headache.

VOICE: *(O S)* Don't be silly. It's good for you. Soothing.

MARTIN: It makes me anxious.

VOICE: *(O S)* Everything makes you anxious.

MARTIN: I make my own music.

VOICE: *(O S)* I'm not sure that's music. This is the real deal. Classical.

MARTIN: I HATE IT! IT'S LIKE RAZOR BLADES IN MY EARS!

VOICE: *(O S)* You really are wound up today.

MARTIN: I have headache. This was all a mistake. Take her away. I don't want to be a father.

VOICE: *(O S)* You don't mean that.

MARTIN: It's too much responsibility.

VOICE: *(O S)* Don't be silly.

MARTIN: I'd rather be a composer. I want to be an artist.

VOICE: *(O S)* You're just hungry.

MARTIN: I can't do it. With her.

VOICE: *(O S)* You need cake. And you, Sheila? What do you need? A nice Chardonnay? That always makes me feel better.

ESTHER: I'll find a way out. I'm not as stupid as this guy.

MARTIN: See?

VOICE: *(O S)* That would be a waste of your time. You are the reward of years of hard work and persistence. We could never just let you go.

ESTHER: I'll die here. Please. I don't mind begging. I'll beg all day.

VOICE: *(O S)* We won't let you die. Now, everyone take a deep breath. We got off to a bad start. It happens. Martin, ask her about herself, and don't do anything gross. I'll send in the food. We'll get this all sorted out. I promise.

MARTIN: I'm going to poop on her head.

VOICE: *(O S)* Martin. You want that cake?

(The sound of a mic rustling)

(MARTIN takes a seat at his piano. He plays a familiar, happy tune. Kermit's Rainbow Connection *or something of the sort.)*

(As MARTIN sings ESTHER physically searches for any exit she can imagine. Throwing herself at walls. Anything)

(MARTIN continues with his happy song until finally ESTHER takes her rage toward MARTIN and tears off his suit.)

(He's wearing simple underwear underneath.)

(She throws the suit aside.)

MARTIN: What did you have to do that for?

ESTHER: Heaven forbid he live alone. Without someone to carry his fucking name. Bear his child. And I get to live my life, as I wish. Without question. Without judgement. Free.

MARTIN: Who's judging you? No one even knew you existed until last week.

ESTHER: They should have killed me when they found me. Just like they should have killed you. LET US DIE! LET US DIE!

MARTIN: I don't want to die.

ESTHER: Let us end. Enjoy our extinction in a flaming ball of freedom.

MARTIN: I don't want to end.

ESTHER: The planet's dying anyway.

MARTIN: No it's not.

ESTHER: They're killing it.

MARTIN: No.

ESTHER: Oh, they didn't tell you that? *(Silence)* We're just the canary in the coal mine.

MARTIN: Canary? What coal mine?

VOICE: *(O S)* Here we go!

(A ridiculous heaping tray of food of every kind—a feast—gets pushed from off stage, on a large cart.)

MARTIN: She's crazy.

VOICE: *(O S)* Martin.

MARTIN: You should hear the things she's saying.

VOICE: *(O S)* When a man say that a woman is crazy, it usually only proves that he himself is the one unhinged, difficult, and manipulative. Usually a liar. Take my husband, for example. He called me crazy twice this morning.

MARTIN: But she *is* crazy.

VOICE: *(O S)* Where's your suit?

MARTIN: She tore it off me!

VOICE: *(O S)* That wasn't very nice.

ESTHER: I'll kill him before I'll let him touch me.

MARTIN: See?

VOICE: *(O S)* You both need to eat something. I'm hell on wheels when I'm hungry.

(MARTIN rushes for the food. He piles food on a plate.)

(ESTHER watches him.)

VOICE: *(O S)* Martin. Small portions.

MARTIN: I'm not going to let it go to waste.

VOICE: *(O S)* Your mouth is not a garbage can.

(ESTHER kicks around some of MARTIN's stuff.)

MARTIN: Hey, that's mine. *(To GINA)* See? Bonkers.

VOICE: *(O S)* Sheila is just tired and cranky. It's been a long day.

MARTIN: My failed wife's name is Esther.

VOICE: *(O S)* We like Sheila better. And she's not failed. No one has failed. Everything takes time.

MARTIN: *(Eating)* You might have failed, Gina.

VOICE: *(O S)* No.

MARTIN: Maybe.

VOICE: *(O S)* No.

MARTIN: I know how you hate that.

VOICE: *(O S)* I didn't fail. We haven't failed.

MARTIN: Oh now it's *we*?

VOICE: *(O S)* Eat your dinner. Martin.

ESTHER: If you are determined to keep me here against my will, Lady, I want some real furniture and bedding. And, I want some lizards.

VOICE: *(O S)* That stuff is real.

ESTHER: You guessing you found this crap at Walmart and thought he'd like it.

VOICE: *(O S)* He does.

(ESTHER *looks at* MARTIN. *He's gorging himself.*)

MARTIN: It's fine.

ESTHER: I want lizards.

VOICE: *(O S)* I'm not putting lizards in there.

ESTHER: Why not?

VOICE: *(O S)* You don't belong in the same study.

ESTHER: Says who?

VOICE: *(O S)* Everyone. You don't need lizards in there. You have Martin.

(MARTIN *smiles with huge bite of food in his mouth.*)

ESTHER: If you want me to even consider—*consider*—and when I say consider, I mean let it sit on my brain for one second without gagging—touching this bloated specimen you're so desperate to mate—I need lizards.

VOICE: *(O S)* Why?

ESTHER: They're my community.

MARTIN: *(Through the food in his mouth)* It's water weight.

VOICE: *(O S)* Lizards are not in my field of study.

MARTIN: She's a frog woman.

VOICE: *(O S)* Martin.

MARTIN: Person. Frog person.

VOICE: *(O S)* That's not my point—

ESTHER: I don't care what kind of person you are. You yanked me away from my home, my life, and a really great group of friends, and being our frog community has all been destroyed by people like you, my friends have been lizards. Kind and patient lizards.

VOICE: *(O S)* I don't know lizards.

ESTHER: Learn. *(Silence)* If you want your so-called study to succeed, you need for me to be happy. Content. Thriving. Among those whose company I enjoy. *(Silence)* Just like you.

MARTIN: Gina doesn't have friends.

VOICE: *(O S)* I do too.

MARTIN: Name one?

(Silence)

ESTHER: I'll die if I'm unhappy. And I'll kill him too.

MARTIN: Stop saying that.

VOICE: *(O S)* Have you tried to be happy here, Sheila? Martin had an adjustment period.

ESTHER: You broke his leg.

VOICE: *(O S)* He did that to himself.

MARTIN: Technically.

(ESTHER finally takes a seat.)

ESTHER: Listen, we can go back and forth on this topic all day—you want this, I want that. I want freedom and autonomy. You want fame and recognition. I want the life I had. You want the life you dream of. I fear convention. You fear loneliness. I value adventure. You value security. I want to live as I please. You want to please, honor, and obey. I have seen my people destroyed. You are the destroyer. I see the truth. You see what you want to see. Potato. Tomato. Radish. Radicchio. So, let me just put it this way: I will rip his heart out with my teeth and then kill myself with the leg of one of these chairs in a murder suicide scene that would be too bloody and brutal and graphic for even Dateline to cover, if you don't put some lizards in here.

(Silence)

VOICE: *(O S)* What kind of lizard?

ESTHER: Lizards.

VOICE: *(O S)* You get one.

ESTHER: Two.

VOICE: *(O S)* One, and that's my final offer.

ESTHER: Two. Or I rip his heart out and kill myself while you watch.

MARTIN: Gina.

ESTHER: I'm not kidding. You don't know what I've done to survive out there. It takes a lot to be the Last in the Kingdom. The Only One. A Woman Like No Other. Frog Queen.

MARTIN: Who said you were all that?

ESTHER: I did.

(Silence)

VOICE: *(O S)* I'll see what I can do.

MARTIN: Gina!

ESTHER: And don't you dare go to a pet store and try and throw some of those guys in here. *(Pointing to* MARTIN*)* You take all the joy and fun out of anyone when you do this to him.

VOICE: *(O S)* I'm not making any promises.

MARTIN: Gina?!

ESTHER: And get me some real atmosphere in here. Lilies. Flowers. Give me something to live for.

VOICE: *(O S)* You really are asking a lot—

ESTHER: You want me to touch that? Your prized specimen?

*(*MARTIN *is licking his fingers.)*

ESTHER: You do want to succeed, don't you Lady PhD? *(Silence)* You want people to appreciate all your hard work. Your research.

(Silence)

VOICE: *(O S)* I'll see what I can do.

(The rustle of the mic)

MARTIN: Please don't kill me.

ESTHER: All the years I thought it would be nice to have a lover, of my own kind, and one day with you and I see I've missed nothing.

MARTIN: The music.

ESTHER: Uh huh.

MARTIN: She's not going to put lizards in here. She says she's going to do things, and then never does. Like win a Nobel prize. Or leave her husband.

ESTHER: I can be persuasive.

MARTIN: What if she does get you your lizards and they eat me? Or you?

ESTHER: Lizards are Pacifist.

MARTIN: I've never heard that.

ESTHER: Like Mennonites.

MARTIN: Really?

ESTHER: A lot like Mennonites. Kind. Patient. They sing when they're sad. They took me in to their fold, as one of their own.

MARTIN: I like the singing part.

ESTHER: I could be a little rough for them.

MARTIN: What if they're girls and they fall in love with me? Won't you be jealous?

ESTHER: No.

MARTIN: Are you sure? Jealousy is pretty tricky.

ESTHER: What do you know about jealousy?

MARTIN: Gina hacks her husband emails.

ESTHER: Rest assured. *(She inspects the food.)* They call this food?

MARTIN: What's wrong with it?

ESTHER: It's dead.

MARTIN: How else are we supposed to eat it?

ESTHER: Have you ever tasted a live cricket on your tongue? That's joy. Tasting it's blood in your mouth. It's legs kick that last kick. Then surrender…that's bliss.

MARTIN: I'm trying to find qualities that I like about you.

ESTHER: My hair.

MARTIN: I try to keep a positive spirt, and I see that's not important to you. This was a peaceful place before you came. A sanctuary. And now look at it? Look at me? *(He pops some food in his mouth.)*

ESTHER: It's a glass box with some water and cheap shit thrown in here to try and make you feel like you're not living for nothing.

MARTIN: Well it was working just fine. Now I feel, I'm starting to feel all messed up inside. Uneasy. Bordering on existentially confused. *(He sits down. Takes a bag of chips with him.)* You're the worst thing to ever happen to me.

ESTHER: I hate to break it to you, but THIS was the worst thing that happened to you.

MARTIN: Can you please….? It is my home. I thought we could at least be friends. I was excited for the company.

ESTHER: I was free! Don't you understand that?! Free.

MARTIN: I didn't do it.

ESTHER: Your existence did.

MARTIN: Well then, I'm sorry. *(Silence)* I would never want to hurt you. I am a Christian.

ESTHER: Uh huh.

MARTIN: You don't have any spiritual beliefs?

ESTHER: Depends.

MARTIN: On what?

ESTHER: How close to death I am.

MARTIN: There's something very dangerous about you.

ESTHER: Thank you.

MARTIN: All the things I thought we might do together, are just... And I'm not talking just sexy things. Though I did think we'd do that a lot. With steady, frequent, vigorous abandon. There were other things I was looking forward to as well.

ESTHER: Like what?

MARTIN: Long talks. Writing songs together. Laughs. Charades. I've never played and Gina was talking about it one day, and I thought it sounded fun.

ESTHER: Gina has zero imagination.

MARTIN: You don't even know her.

ESTHER: We're in this mess because of women and men, like Gina, who think that everyone needs a mate and a family to survive. To save the world.

MARTIN: Maybe she's right.

ESTHER: If you're coming out of World War Two, maybe you need to believe that. You've gotta believe in something better being made together after all that death and destruction. But now? Come on. It's so 1950s, it's embarrassing.

MARTIN: Isn't there still a lot of death?

ESTHER: Making women have babies isn't the answer. Just because you sell it to them as their destiny, does not make it true. It's a fantasy. A dream. A nightmare.

MARTIN: You lost me.

ESTHER: Because you are brain-washed by this dream, my friend.

MARTIN: Personally, I think this is how we're supposed to live.

ESTHER: Trapped?

MARTIN: Safe. With love.

ESTHER: Trapped.

MARTIN: You and me, we've been doing it all wrong. Alone.

ESTHER: I was happy.

MARTIN: She doth protest too much. Gina has a similar problem.

ESTHER: Gina has more than one problem.

MARTIN: True. She lives on Xanax. But, she's got three kids she loves. Patty, Polly, and Peter. A stay-at-home husband named William. Billy, when she's in a good mood.

ESTHER: And she tells you she's happy?

MARTIN: Yes. Often. When she's not crying. We've seen each other through a lot.

ESTHER: But.

MARTIN: What?

ESTHER: But.

MARTIN: What??

ESTHER: Was your childhood happy?

MARTIN: I told you. I don't like to think about it.

ESTHER: But we have to think about it, don't we? We have to. If we are going to have children of our own. *(She finally sits as close as she's gotten to him.)*

(MARTIN flinches.)

ESTHER: What's wrong?

MARTIN: Are you going to kill me?

ESTHER: No.

MARTIN: You're sitting awfully close.

ESTHER: So.

MARTIN: It makes me want you.

ESTHER: Contain yourself.

MARTIN: It's not easy.

(ESTHER scoots her chair back.)

ESTHER: If we don't think about what we went through, how can we consider putting our children through the same thing? Do you really want your kids to grow up in a place like this?

MARTIN: They'd be safe.

ESTHER: Is that all there is now? Safety?

MARTIN: I think so.

ESTHER: I want more.

MARTIN: Everything changes when you have the kids. That's what Gina says.

ESTHER: For you. Not for them. *(She looks around the room.)* This is a prison, Martin.

(MARTIN looks around.)

MARTIN: Some days. Maybe. But I call it home. *(He smiles.)* I have my music.

ESTHER: It makes me want to cry for you.

MARTIN: Please don't. If you start, I'll start, and once I start, I can't stop.

ESTHER: No fresh air. Only vents. A small opening at the top. *(She keeps her eyes on the ceiling.)* I hope she brings those lizards.

MARTIN: I don't. Where will we put them?

ESTHER: Does it get dark every night in here?

MARTIN: Of course.

ESTHER: They go home?

MARTIN: Yes.

ESTHER: I've got plans for you and me.

MARTIN: Sex?

ESTHER: No.

MARTIN: Will it be painful?

(ESTHER keeps her eyes on the ceiling.)

(Sounds of the forest)

Scene 2

(ESTHER pulls in new furniture. Plants. Work-out equipment)

ESTHER: You heard me. Put them in here.

VOICE: *(O S)* What do you need ropes for?

ESTHER: Exercise.

VOICE: *(O S)* But—

ESTHER: Hammock building.

VOICE: *(O S)* Look at all this stuff you already have. It's too much.

ESTHER: You want me to be happy? With him. *(She yanks the ropes inside.)* Now get me those lizards.

VOICE: *(O S)* I'm trying. They run really fast.

ESTHER: Try harder, Lady.

VOICE: *(O S)* You're too bossy. I don't like it.

ESTHER: You're lazy.

VOICE: *(O S)* That is one thing I am not.

ESTHER: Then where are the lizards?

(MARTIN is at the piano.)

MARTIN: *(Singing)*
When you dream of love, and companionship…what do you get?
Esther K…
When you think your world is about to change, and all your dreams are met,
What do you get instead?
Esther K…
She won't touch you
She says your breath is a cess pool, and your body gross
She tells you she will kill you day and night, and you haven't slept in months
Your life is hell, but you still want
Esther K…
Esther K…
Esther K…
Please, is there anything I can do to move your heart?

ESTHER: No.

MARTIN: *(Singing)*
Can I at least touch your body?

ESTHER: No.

MARTIN: *(Singing)*
Your hand?

ESTHER: No.

MARTIN: *(Singing)*
Your finger tip?

ESTHER: No.

MARTIN: *(Singing)*
Your foot?

ESTHER: No.

MARTIN: *(Singing)*
The webbing in between your toes?

ESTHER: No.

MARTIN: *(Singing)*
Esther K....

(ESTHER *keeps pulling in the ropes. Looking around the room. Planning.)*

Scene 3

(ESTHER *is lifting weights.)*

MARTIN: *(Singing)*
I had a simple life.
And now it's not so simple...
I don't know what it is, but it's not mine....
Was it ever really mine in the first place?

(GERALD *and* RUTH *enter slowly. They scan the room with their eyes. Stunned)*

VOICE: *(O S)* Hey, Sheila. Are you happy now?

MARTIN: Have you been drinking?

VOICE: *(O S)* No.

MARTIN: *(Singing)*
Lizards!

(RUTH is carrying a large heavy baby in a blanket. All we see are large blinking eyes peeking out.)

(GERALD wears a small back pack.)

VOICE: *(O S)* Meet Danny and Ginger. Martin and Sheila, Danny and Ginger, Ginger and Danny, Martin and Sheila.

(ESTHER drops the weights.)

ESTHER: Oh. Great. Finally. *(She wipes her hands on her pants. Goes in for the hug)* Welcome! My name's Esther. And you are?

(Silence)

RUTH: Ruth.

ESTHER: I'm sorry, what was that?

RUTH: Ruth.

ESTHER: I still didn't get it.

RUTH: RUTH.

ESTHER: Oh. Ruth.

RUTH: Yes. Nice to meet you.

GERALD: Gerald.

ESTHER: Gerald. Nice to meet you. I'm so glad to see you both.

VOICE: *(O S)* What did they say? Speak up, please. We like Danny and Ginger.

RUTH: What's that smell?

ESTHER: That's him. Martin.

MARTIN: No.

GERALD: Who is he?

MARTIN: Martin.

ESTHER: The culprit.

MARTIN: I prefer subject.

ESTHER: Culprit.

GERALD: Of?

MARTIN: Research.

RUTH: I don't like the sound of that. Oh dear. I've heard about that. Do they poke you?

MARTIN: No.

GERALD: What kind of research?

RUTH: Oh dear.

MARTIN: I'm the last male frog of my kind. She, is the last female. We are supposed to reproduce and change the world, and but she, won't have me. Or said she wouldn't have me until she got some lizards in here.

ESTHER: Oh, we'll get to that. I bet you all are tired and hungry. Lady, can we get some food in here?

VOICE: *(O S)* I don't work for you.

ESTHER: I think you do. If you want results. Food. Now. Please.

RUTH: I need to sit down. "Research." *(She looks for a place to rest.)* This has been a very trying experience. Very trying indeed. Oh my. What a day.

ESTHER: There's a place right here.

MARTIN: That's my bed.

RUTH: I don't want to put anyone out. I don't like to be a bother.

ESTHER: No. Please. You can take it.

RUTH: Are you sure?

ESTHER: Please.

RUTH: Thank you. Oh my. *(She sits. Baby in arms. Heavy)* What a day indeed. Goodness. I think I've lost my hat.

MARTIN: Watch my stuff. You're sitting on my maps.

RUTH: Am I? Oh dear. I'm sorry. I do miss my hat.

ESTHER: Pick them up, Martin.

MARTIN: I guess everything's going to change. Once again. Oh, the halcyon days of my bachelor youth.

RUTH: I'll try not to disturb them. I don't want to be a bother.

(MARTIN moves close to the baby.)

MARTIN: Oh hello there little one. She's got a kid with her, Esther.

ESTHER: I see that.

MARTIN: Some folks aren't against it. Boy or girl?

RUTH: Girl.

MARTIN: What?

ESTHER: Girl.

MARTIN: Cute. What's her name?

RUTH: Lily.

MARTIN: I want children. Badly. Esther here hates them.

ESTHER: Not true.

MARTIN: Kid's kind of old for that blanket, don't you think?

RUTH: Well, she's not like other children.

MARTIN: What do you mean?

RUTH: Some people think it was the water. I don't know. I just don't know. It tasted fine.

MARTIN: What?

RUTH: She needs extra care and attention. Protection.

MARTIN: I see.

RUTH: She'll be eaten if I set her down.

MARTIN: Yikes.

RUTH: It's quite stressful, keeping her safe. But I wouldn't change a thing about her. She's perfect.

MARTIN: Can she walk?

RUTH: Not yet. *(She pushes a smile.)* I try to hold her at all times. Just in case.

MARTIN: Wow.

RUTH: But she is getting bigger. I don't know how much longer I can carry her. *(She pushes a smile.)* What a day.

VOICE: *(O S)* It looks a little crowded in there. Are you sure this is going to work out? Sheila?

ESTHER: How about that food? Let's worry about that.

VOICE: *(O S)* I don't like your attitude.

MARTIN: See what I live with? Day in, day out?

VOICE: *(O S)* Oh, stop complaining, Martin. It's unattractive.

MARTIN: Gina?

VOICE: *(O S)* A little help would be nice. I'm working my ass off out here.

(Sound of the mic rustling O S)

GERALD: Can someone please tell me what are we are doing here? Please? I'm very confused.

(ESTHER leans in.)

ESTHER: See that vent?

GERALD: Yes.

ESTHER: You and Ruth can climb.

GERALD: So.

ESTHER: I need your help.

GERALD: You can climb.

ESTHER: Not as high. Not like you two. And he's got a bad leg. I need your help to get us out of here.

RUTH: I have a lot of carry already. As you can see. Not that I mind. I'm just tired. But that is a lot to ask.

ESTHER: You help us get out of here, we all go home.

RUTH: I'd hate to seem like I'm complaining. Does it sound like I'm complaining?

GERALD: Why us? I'm trying to understand. Do you know her, Ruth?

RUTH: No.

GERALD: *(To* RUTH*)* My heart is still racing.

RUTH: Mine too. But mine often races.

ESTHER: Long story short, as you just heard, all my people are all gone, except for him.

(MARTIN *pushes a smile.)*

ESTHER: So I must ask for help from your community.

GERALD: Our community?

ESTHER: Lizards. I lived with lizards. Most of my life.

MARTIN: I don't like all these schemes and secrets. I'm staying here.

RUTH: Secrets are terrible. Unless necessary. Sometimes they're necessary.

(GERALD *begins to follow* ESTHER *around the room.)*

GERALD: I'm sorry, please, let me just get this straight. I'm still trying to understand.

RUTH: It's very confusing.

GERALD: One minute I'm minding my own business, walking my son to school, and the next I'm yanked from his hand, pulled by my legs and arms as he cries and runs toward me, and rushed to this, I don't even know what to call it—

MARTIN: I call it my condo—

GERALD: Prison.

MARTIN: Well.

GERALD: Simply because you know some lizards back home, and need help getting out of here?

ESTHER: That is one way to put it. But I wouldn't call it simple.

(GERALD *stops.*)

GERALD: Why would you do that to us?

ESTHER: I was desperate. I am desperate. I'd do it for you.

GERALD: Really?

ESTHER: If it meant your freedom.

GERALD: Really?

ESTHER: Yes.

GERALD: A stranger?

ESTHER: Yes.

RUTH: Oh dear.

GERALD: You'd give up your own freedom just to save someone you've never met.

ESTHER: Yes.

GERALD: Uh huh.

ESTHER: I would.

RUTH: I'm not sure what I've done to deserve this. I'm a good person. I've raised many children. I've been generous.

ESTHER: This is all temporary. Please. I'm trying to explain. Trust me. We'll be out of here in no time. We just have to wait until dark, when they all go home. I've got it all worked out.

MARTIN: I'm staying.

ESTHER: That's your choice.

MARTIN: I like it here.

RUTH: Really? I think it's dreadful. It's very bright. I don't like to complain, but it seems very bright. *(She covers the baby's eyes.)* I do wish I had my hat.

ESTHER: What part of the forest are you from? I bet we know lots of people in common. Do you know Rick and Nancy?

GERALD: No.

ESTHER: Carol and Jim?

GERALD: No.

ESTHER: Bart and Bobby?

GERALD: No.

ESTHER: Doug and Brenda.

RUTH: Brenda's my cousin.

ESTHER: I love Brenda! She's a good friend of mine.

RUTH: I'm sorry, what is your name again?

ESTHER: Esther.

RUTH: *(Thinking)* I've never heard of you. No. I don't recall an Esther.

ESTHER: Well—

RUTH: Brenda and I don't speak very often. I have a lot of responsibilities, as you might imagine, and she sleeps until all hours of the day.

ESTHER: She does like a party.

RUTH: Yes. It must be nice.. Not that I'm judging. Each to her own. I just wouldn't know what it was like to have all that time on my hands.

ESTHER: Are you two together?

RUTH: Us? No. Neighbors. He has a husband. Larry.

ESTHER: Pardon me.

RUTH: Just bad luck we were in the same place, at the same time, I guess. Right, Gerald? A nice rock next to the river. Distracted by the sun. It was right in my eyes when they caught me.

GERALD: A nightmare.

RUTH: I didn't know what was happening. Gerald has been very strong and helpful. I have a lot on my plate. As you can see. And now this? Goodness. I'm not complaining.

GERALD: You've been very brave, Ruth.

RUTH: Thank you. That means a lot. I do what I can. *(She kisses the baby's head.)* I try and set a good example. We have to, you know, for the children.

ESTHER: Please, I understand how you're both feeling.

GERALD: I'm not sure you do.

ESTHER: I've been there. I'm still there. Look at us? What is this? Who lives like this?

MARTIN: I like it.

ESTHER: I am desperate to get out of here, and desperate times call for desperate measures—

MARTIN: That's a good country song. *(He sits at the piano. Singing)*
Desperate times and desperate measures...
What does it all add up to?

ESTHER: Not now, Martin

MARTIN: *(Singing)*
The lizards have arrived and now they're angry and
   sad
Who does Esther think she is?
Stealing freedom from other people
Everyone thinks she's bad...

VOICE: *(O S)* Supper's on! Ding ding ding!

(A heaping cart of food is pushed in.)

VOICE: *(O S)* This should be plenty for everyone.

(MARTIN rushes for the food.)

VOICE: *(O S)* Martin, don't be greedy. And Sheila?

ESTHER: What?

VOICE: *(O S)* We had a deal. *(Silence)* We had a deal.
Remember?

ESTHER: What deal?

VOICE: *(O S)* Time to start touching Martin. Babies.

MARTIN: Can I eat first?

ESTHER: You can't rush these things.

VOICE: *(O S)* Rush? Rush? Look at all I've done for you.
Catching lizards is a lot harder than frogs. These two
were pure luck.

RUTH: It was the sun. It was very bright. Right in my
eyes. I lost my hat.

VOICE: *(O S)* We had a deal. Two lizards. Your
happiness. Now, let's see some action with Martin.

MARTIN: Can I finish my dinner?

ESTHER: I can't.

VOICE: *(O S)* Do it.

ESTHER: I want to be in love.

VOICE: *(O S)* Love? No. No. We had a deal.

ESTHER: I need to be in love. Deep, passionate love. Sorry.

VOICE: *(O S)* No you don't. My last two kids were made in a petri dish.

(RUTH *joins* MARTIN *and looks over the food, impressed.*)

RUTH: They feed you here?

MARTIN: Every day.

RUTH: Really?

MARTIN: Really.

RUTH: Oh my goodness. Silver linings show up in the strangest places, I guess. Gerald, do you see this food?

(GERALD *is looking around the room, shaking his head.*)

RUTH: Gerald?

MARTIN: Sometimes I ask for seconds.

RUTH: No.

MARTIN: Yes.

RUTH: And they give it to you?

MARTIN: Yes. When I was young, Gina used to feed my by hand. She's got a lot invested in me.

RUTH: Who's Gina?

MARTIN: The voice.

RUTH: I don't think I like her.

MARTIN: Her heart is in the right place. She basically raised me.

RUTH: Really?

MARTIN: But now we're like an old married couple.
Weird.

RUTH: This really is quite the feast. Gerald?

(GERALD *doesn't answer.*)

MARTIN: Every night.

RUTH: I can't believe it. Oh my.

MARTIN: Believe it. I don't know what this stuff is right
here, but it's to die for. Try it.

RUTH: I will. It's just, the baby—

MARTIN: And this. Kind of sweet and sour.

RUTH: Is it alive?

MARTIN: No. Gross. No.

RUTH: Oh. Well. Let me make a plate. Gerald? *(Silence)*
Gerald? Do you hear me?

(GERALD *takes off his small backpack. Holds it close to his
chest. It's clearly his son's.*)

RUTH: Aren't you hungry? It's been a long day.

GERALD: No.

RUTH: Is there anything I can do?

GERALD: No.

RUTH: It's been a terrible day, but you have to eat, dear.
You must keep your strength up.

(GERALD *nods.*)

RUTH: You did everything you could today. I know
you did. And you helped us, right there next to you. If
it weren't for us, you might have gotten free.

GERALD: That's not what matters—

RUTH: I know, but it is something your family would
be proud of.

GERALD: I just can't understand why someone would steal me from my life, just to save herself.

ESTHER: I had to.

GERALD: It's so selfish. *(He slumps to the floor.)* So terribly selfish.

RUTH: You're not that kind of person. I know.

ESTHER: I had to!

VOICE: *(O S)* What's happening in there? Is he sick? I can barely hear anything. Lizards speak so softly. Speak up!

RUTH: Gerald, we have to be strong.

GERALD: It just doesn't make sense.

RUTH: I know, but you have to be strong, dear. For your son.

GERALD: His little face. His hands, reaching for me. What must he be thinking? Is he scared? My husband. Are they looking for me?

ESTHER: You'll see them again.

GERALD: You don't know that.

ESTHER: I do.

GERALD: How?

ESTHER: Trust me.

MARTIN: She thinks she's some kind of big shot. The Frog Queen. *(Snorts)* Yeah. Right.

RUTH: Gerald. You have to be strong.

GERALD: It's just so terribly selfish.

RUTH: *(Singing the hymn, "Abide With Me")*
Abide with me, fast falls the eventide;
The darkness deepens, Lord with me abide.
When other helpers fail and comforts flee,
Help of the helpless, O abide with me..."

(RUTH *grabs* GERALD's *hand. He joins in the song.*)

RUTH & GERALD: *(Singing)*
Swift to its close ebbs out life's little day;
Earth's joys grow dim; its glories pass away;
Change and decay in all around I see;
O Thou who changest not, abide with me...

GERALD: *(Singing)*
I need Thy presence every passing hour.
What but Thy grace can foil the tempter's power?
Who, like Thyself, my guide and stay can be?
Through cloud and sunshine, Lord, abide with me....

MARTIN: That's catchy. You write that?

ESTHER: I have a plan. I promise you, Gerald. Ruth. Please. You have to trust me.

GERALD: Why should I?

ESTHER: Because we need each other. We all need each other. Here and out there.

GERALD: It's no excuse.

ESTHER: I'm not making an excuse.

GERALD: This is a nightmare. Look at this place? *(He puts his heads in his hands.)*

VOICE: *(O S)* What's going on in there? No one looks happy. What's wrong?

MARTIN: Esther is pissing everyone off, or making them sad.

VOICE: *(O S)* That's not the plan. She said she needed them to be happy.

MARTIN: She still thinks she's going to get out of here.

VOICE: *(O S)* No.

MARTIN: That's what I said.

VOICE: *(O S)* Well, we all need dreams.

(RUTH *wants to get some food, and looks for a place to put the baby, but is unsure.* GERALD *is in his own world.* MARTIN *is eating.*)

RUTH: Oh dear.

ESTHER: What?

RUTH: I want to get some food, but I'm not sure it's safe. Where to put Lily. Goodness.

ESTHER: I can hold her.

(RUTH *examines* ESTHER.)

ESTHER: What?

RUTH: Will you eat her?

ESTHER: Eat her? No. Of course not.

RUTH: How can I trust you? Especially considering we've learned we're in this mess because of you. I'm not complaining, mind you, but this just seems obvious.

ESTHER: I don't have to hold her, but I thought I'd offer. To give you a break.

(*Silence*)

RUTH: My arms are tired.

MARTIN: She hates kids.

ESTHER: No I don't. (*To* RUTH) That's not true.

RUTH: My arms really could use a rest. I'm not complaining.

ESTHER: I'm here if you need me.

RUTH: I am hungry. Well…I guess she'll be safe. Will she be safe?

ESTHER: Yes.

(RUTH *finally places the baby in* ESTHER'*s arms.*)

RUTH: Just for a little while. I'm very hungry.

ESTHER: She's lighter than I expected.

RUTH: It's hard to find food for both of us. Everyone's always waiting for me to drop her. I see them staring at us. Waiting. Waiting to eat her.

ESTHER: That sounds miserable.

RUTH: I'm not complaining. It's just a lot. I love her so.

ESTHER: She's got a sweet face.

RUTH: Doesn't she?

ESTHER: I've got her. Really. Get some food.

RUTH: I just need a rest sometimes.

ESTHER: You can trust me.

RUTH: I really try not to complain. We all have our gifts and burdens.

ESTHER: Of course.

RUTH: Are you sure she is safe with you?

ESTHER: I promise.

RUTH: I can't help but worry. I worry all the time.

(RUTH joins MARTIN at the feast. Enthused by someone who is excited by his menu, he piles food on a plate for her.)

RUTH: Oh my.

MARTIN: Best buffet in town.

RUTH: It is impressive.

VOICE: (O S) How does that feel, Sheila?

ESTHER: What?

VOICE: (O S) The baby?

ESTHER: You know my name is Esther.

VOICE: (O S) How does that feel?

ESTHER: What?

VOICE: (O S) The baby.

(ESTHER *looks at the large eyes of the baby. The pull of it's
weight in her arms.*)

VOICE: *(O S)* You can have that too now. Your own
child. *(Silence)* I know you had given all this up, the
possibility, the love. But, this is your chance. It's your
last and *only* chance to be a mother. To know what it
feels like to carry a child. To feel it kick inside you.
To give birth. *(Silence)* All those years and years you
thought it was impossible, and now, like magic, here
you are, you have the chance to feel it for yourself.
With Martin. You can have something you never
thought you would be able to have. Never. And yet,
here its is. Your last chance to enjoy the simple yet
profound pleasure of motherhood.

ESTHER: It's not simple.

VOICE: *(O S)* But haven't you wondered, who you
would be as a mother? What would it feel like? What
kind of person would I be? What kind of child would
I have? Oh, the things you would learn about yourself
that you never knew possible.

ESTHER: No.

VOICE: *(O S)* How to be selfless. Truly selfless. The
parts of you that you never knew existed. And the
love. The love. The love. Love like no other.

ESTHER: It's not for everyone.

VOICE: *(O S)* But it can be for you now. It can. Martin
can give you that. He can give you something you let
go of long ago. Now, you'll be complete. Fulfill your
purpose.

ESTHER: I am complete.

VOICE: *(O S)* Please.

ESTHER: I want love.

VOICE: *(O S)* That's love right there. Look at her.

ESTHER: Not this kind.

VOICE: *(O S)* The child will be the love.

ESTHER: It's not enough.

VOICE: *(O S)* It could be.

ESTHER: Not for me.

VOICE: *(O S)* It could be enough. You've never tried it.

ESTHER: And I want my freedom.

VOICE: *(O S)* You've had that.

ESTHER: I need my freedom.

VOICE: *(O S)* Freedom is overrated.

ESTHER: It's everything.

VOICE: *(O S)* It's selfish.

ESTHER: It's better than love.

VOICE: *(O S)* Why are you crying?

ESTHER: Stop it.

VOICE: *(O S)* Does this make you sad?

ESTHER: Why do we hear your voice?

VOICE: *(O S)* I'm in control.

ESTHER: I don't want to hear you.

VOICE: *(O S)* I'm in control. We are all in control of you. That's just the way it is.

ESTHER: No.

VOICE: *(O S)* Yes. And we want you to be a mother.

ESTHER: It's my life.

VOICE: *(O S)* Motherhood could be everything you ever wanted, you just don't know it yet. The future depends on you, remember. It's your job.

ESTHER: It's my life.

VOICE: *(O S)* Not really.

ESTHER: Knock it off.

VOICE: *(O S)* You're so small, compared to me.

ESTHER: Knock it off.

VOICE: *(O S)* This is your last chance. To know the greatest gift of all.

ESTHER: I said, knock it off.

VOICE: *(O S)* My voice is your voice too. Isn't it?

ESTHER: No.

VOICE: *(O S)* Sheila. Please.

ESTHER: I'm not going to yell in this child's ear, but if you don't knock it off, I will walk over there right now and finally give Martin the fatal blow to his brains I've been promising.

MARTIN: What?

(GERALD, RUTH *and* MARTIN *have* ESTHER's *attention.*)

ESTHER: I'm not your pet to play with, like him. I have my own mind.

VOICE: *(O S)* We made a deal.

ESTHER: I don't want to hear one more word out of you.

VOICE: *(O S)* You will still hear me. Won't you?

MARTIN: Gina.

VOICE: *(O S)* We made a deal. I will order him to move on top of you. To take you, whether you want it or not. I need babies. Success.

ESTHER: *(Covering the baby's ears)* QUIET!

MARTIN: This is what I live with now. Shouting.

ESTHER: QUIET!

(RUTH *rushes for her baby.*)

VOICE: *(O S)* Shout all you want but I won't wait much longer.

(The sound of the rain forest)

Scene 4

(Dusk)

(RUTH *holds the baby.)*

ESTHER: We need to wait just a little while longer. And then, everyone goes home.

(MARTIN *is at the piano. Tinkering)*

MARTIN: *(Singing)*
It's not going to work, Esther K….

RUTH: Don't we have far to go? It seems like it was forever until we got here.

MARTIN: *(Singing)*
Too far…that's why I'm not going…too far…

RUTH: I'm not complaining, but it was far. That's a fact.

MARTIN: *(Singing)*
"It's a fact…"

ESTHER: Look at Martin's maps. It's not that far. We can make it.

MARTIN: *(Singing)*
Those don't mean anything.

ESTHER: You can lead a frog out of the river, but you can't take the river out of the frog.

MARTIN: *(Singing)*
I've never heard that…

ESTHER: It's true. Its in our blood.

MARTIN: *(Singing)*
You're just making that up to make us feel better and convince us to risk our lives for you—

*(*GERALD *stands beside* MARTIN.*)*

GERALD: Do you mind?

MARTIN: You play?

GERALD: I can't stand to hear you sing anymore. Or whatever it is you do.

MARTIN: Oh.

GERALD: It's too much.

*(*MARTIN *steps aside.)*

MARTIN: Hint taken.

*(*GERALD *sits down at the piano, not to play, but to prevent* MARTIN *from any ideas.)*

MARTIN: You like it out there?

GERALD: Where?

MARTIN: The forest.

GERALD: It's home.

MARTIN: Esther says they're killing it.

GERALD: This is true.

MARTIN: Really?

GERALD: Yes.

MARTIN: What's everyone going to do?

GERALD: I don't know. *(Silence)* I try not to think about it too often. Have some faith. *(Silence)* Enjoy the good things.

MARTIN: Does that work?

GERALD: Most days. *(He holds his son's backpack.)*

MARTIN: What's it like to be a Dad?

GERALD: Pardon?

MARTIN: What's it like to be a father? Do you like it?

GERALD: Oh yes. It's wonderful. I love it.

MARTIN: Really?

GERALD: Yes.

MARTIN: Is it the control? You like having control over someone else?

GERALD: No. Not at all.

MARTIN: Do you have a picture?

(GERALD *searches his pocket. Finds a small photo on a leaf, and hands it to* MARTIN.)

MARTIN: He's cute. Looks just like you.

GERALD: So I've been told. (*He looks at the photo himself, then puts the photo away.*) My son is the best thing to ever happen to me. Next to my husband.

MARTIN: Why?

GERALD: He shows me things I would have never noticed before.

MARTIN: Like what?

GERALD: Oh, everything. He's very perceptive. Everything is new in his eyes. Little specks of dew on a branch. The sky. The moon. Birds passing overhead. He's very curious.

MARTIN: Wow.

RUTH: He's a lovely boy. Just lovely.

GERALD: Thank you, Ruth.

RUTH: He's always been very kind to Lily.

GERALD: That's how he is.

RUTH: He really is. Very mature. Everyone is very fond of him. His name is Eric.

MARTIN: Eric.

RUTH: He's a wonderful boy.

MARTIN: I'd like a son.

GERALD: It's very stressful.

RUTH: Keeping them alive.

GERALD: Yes. Every day.

RUTH: It's a full time job. Not that I'm complaining. But it's a lot.

GERALD: What will happen to them? Will they survive?

RUTH: Oh it's a very stressful indeed. *(Silence)* Chin up, Gerald.

GERALD: *(Singing* I'll Fly Away)
Some bright morning when this life is over
I'll fly away
To that home on God's celestial shore
I'll fly away

(RUTH *joins in the singing.)*

GERALD & RUTH: *(Singing)*
I'll fly away, oh glory
I'll fly away in the morning
When I die, Hallelujah by and by
I'll fly away

(ESTHER *joins in the singing.)*

GERALD, RUTH & ESTHER: *(Singing)*
When the shadows of this life have gone
I'll fly away
Like a bird from these prison walls I'll fly
I'll fly away

I'll fly away, oh glory
I'll fly away in the morning
When I die, Hallelujah by and by
I'll fly away"

(Silence)

GERALD: I hope I see him again.

ESTHER: You will.

RUTH: You have to be strong.

MARTIN: Another catchy tune. You lizards have a lot of them.

GERALD: I may be a Pacifist—

RUTH: That's just our way.

GERALD: But I'll kill you, Esther, if we don't get home. It's a crime what you've done to us. Ruth and I don't deserve this. It's too much to ask of any "community". Or us.

ESTHER: I know.

GERALD: It's too much. To be stolen.

(Silence)

ESTHER: I know. I'm sorry.

(Sounds of the rainforest)

ESTHER: I am thanking you with all my heart, and my life, in advance.

Scene 5

(Just a small bit of light)

(ESTHER, MARTIN and RUTH stand looking up.)

ESTHER: Gerald, how's it going up there? *(Silence)* Gerald?

GERALD: *(O S)* I've almost got it open.

ESTHER: Good, good. *(She waits.)* Gerald?

GERALD: *(O S)* No. Wait. Darn it. It's stuck.

ESTHER: Push harder.

GERALD: *(O S)* I'm trying.

(ESTHER looks up. Waiting)

ESTHER: Can you use your foot?

GERALD: *(O S)* Which foot?

ESTHER: The one you're not using.

GERALD: *(O S)* I don't need your attitude. Esther.

ESTHER: It's an observation.

(They all look up.)

GERALD: *(O S)* I think it's taped shut.

ESTHER: It can't be.

RUTH: Oh dear.

MARTIN: Sounds like something Gina would do.

ESTHER: Push harder.

GERALD: *(O S)* I'm trying....

(They all wait.)

GERALD: *(O S)* Shit.

(They all wait.)

(RUTH prays.)

GERALD: *(O S)* Got it. With my *other* foot.

ESTHER: See? Told you.

GERALD: *(O S)* I'm not amused.

ESTHER: Now can you throw that rope down please.

GERALD: *(O S)* Give me a second. Geez.

(They all look up.)

GERALD: *(O S)* You're too bossy.

MARTIN: Tell me about it.

ESTHER: I call it leadership.

GERALD: *(O S)* I'm sure you do.

(The ropes are thrown down.)

ESTHER: Perfect. Nice work, Gerald. Ruth, want to go up? I can hand you the baby—

RUTH: Oh, I'll go last.

ESTHER: Why?

RUTH: I want to.

ESTHER: Are you sure?

RUTH: Yes. I'll help Martin.

ESTHER: Okay. Martin?

MARTIN: No, no.

ESTHER: C'mon. This is your chance.

MARTIN: I can't.

ESTHER: You can. The rope is for you. I got this goddamn rope for you.

MARTIN: What about Gina? No good-bye?

ESTHER: No.

MARTIN: That doesn't seem nice.

ESTHER: Nice?

MARTIN: She's going to be mad.

ESTHER: So what. See what you've been missing all these years, before it's too late.

MARTIN: I like it here.

ESTHER: It's your last chance to be free.

MARTIN: It sounds so terrible out there. And hot.

ESTHER: It's the price of freedom.

MARTIN: Misery?

ESTHER: Sometimes. Yes.

MARTIN: I'll die.

GERALD: *(O S)* You won't die.

RUTH: Well…

GERALD: *(O S)* Right away.

MARTIN: See!

ESTHER: Someday you're going to die, Martin. See what you've been missing first. Bask in the sun before it's too late.

MARTIN: But my leg. It doesn't work right.

ESTHER: It works good enough. I've seen you run for dinner. And that's what all this rope is for. To pull you up. I'll help you.

MARTIN: For me?

ESTHER: Yes.

MARTIN: That's very thoughtful.

ESTHER: Don't start crying now. We have to go.

MARTIN: I'm touched. But I can't.

(ESTHER grabs MARTIN's face.)

ESTHER: Listen to me, Martin. We, you and me, we are meant to live among the plants and rivers. Rain on our faces. The night sky. The glory of trees above. The fear and exhilaration that comes with living where we belong. On our own terms. Speaking our own language. Free to be who we are..so…please. For this very last time in your life, man…. Ser una frana.

MARTIN: What?

ESTHER: Be a frog.

MARTIN: I'm scared.

ESTHER: Good. *(She goes up the rope.)*

(MARTIN watches ESTHER.)

MARTIN: No. I can't do it.

ESTHER: *(O S)* Come on! Yes you can!

MARTIN: I don't know.

GERALD: *(O S)* You can do it.

MARTIN: Shit.

RUTH: After you.

MARTIN: What about the baby?

RUTH: I've got her. Go.

(MARTIN *looks around at his life.)*

MARTIN: What about my music?

GERALD: *(O S)* Leave it. Please.

(MARTIN *looks around at his life. He makes the decision. Begins to climb the rope, then stops, and climbs back down.)*

ESTHER: *(O S)* No!

(MARTIN *runs and gets his maps and tucks them under his arm.)*

MARTIN: My maps. *(He gives the rope another go.)*

ESTHER: *(O S)* Okay. Slow and steady then. You've got it.

MARTIN: I don't have much upper body strength.

ESTHER: *(O S)* We know.

RUTH: You got it, Martin.

(MARTIN *climbs up.)*

MARTIN: *(O S)* I've got a cramp.

ESTHER: *(O S)* Ready, Ruth?

(RUTH *is now alone. She kisses the baby.)*

GERALD: *(O S)* Ruth?

(RUTH *puts the baby on the bed.)*

RUTH: *(Singing the hymn again,* Abide With Me*)*
"Abide with me, fast falls the eventide,
The darkness deepens; Lord with me abide..."

ESTHER: *(O S)* Ruth?

RUTH: It's for the best, sweetheart. There's plenty of food. It's warm. No one will hurt you.

ESTHER: *(O S)* We need to hurry.

RUTH: Someday you'll understand.

ESTHER: *(O S)* Ruth?

RUTH: Someday.

*(*RUTH *kisses her daughter one last time, and climbs up the rope, helped up by one final tug of* ESTHER's *hand.)*

ESTHER: *(O S)* What about the baby?

MARTIN: *(O S)* What's happening?

GERALD: *(O S)* Ruth?

RUTH: *(O S. Singing)*
When other helpers fail and comforts flee,
Help of the helpless, O abide with me....

(Sounds of the rainforest)

Scene 6

(Morning)

(Lights are turned on, one by one.)

VOICE: *(O S)* Morning everyone. Rise and shine, lizards and toads.

(The room is empty, except for the baby, Lily.)

VOICE: *(O S)* Oh no. No. No. No. Shit on a shingle. *(Silence)* Sheila? Martin? Martin, this isn't funny. Danny? Ginger? *(Silence)* Martin? Martin? No. No. *(Yelling off)* Someone let my goddamn frogs and lizards out…. The frogs and lizards! It's ruined! She ruined everything! Close the windows! Hurry!

(Light on the baby)

VOICE: *(O S)* Oh.

(The baby's eyes blink.)

VOICE: *(O S)* Hello.

(The baby's eyes blink.)

VOICE: *(O S)* So small. Look at you. A little girl. *(Yelling off)* I said, close all the goddamn windows! If it's loose, grab it! This is the thanks I get?! All these years! *(Big sigh)* Stupid Martin. *(Softer, to the baby)* I'm sorry, but…

(The baby's eyes blink.)

VOICE: *(O S)* I don't know much about lizards.

(The eyes blink again.)

VOICE: *(O S)* Though everyone knows, I do love a challenge. *(Big sigh)* I rise to the occasion, I guess. That's who I am. *(Silence)* Oh, look at you. You need help, don't you? *(Silence)* Well. Don't worry.

(Lullaby music plays.)

VOICE: *(O S)* I'll take care of you. I promise. This is a good place for you. Nothing to worry about. This will be your new home. You'll be very happy here. *(Silence)* I think I'll call you Esther. (Without the religious baggage, of course.) *(Silence)* Esthers are smart and brave. Surprising. Successful. *(Yelling off)* Don't stand there staring at me, people! Close the goddamn windows and trap anything running!

(The baby's eyes blink.)

VOICE: *(O S. Softer)* And someday, someday, little Esther, I'll find you a friend. A handsome husband. How about that? You'll have a family. As many babies as you want. It will be so wonderful, and you won't feel alone anymore. Trust me. It will be everything you dreamed.

(The baby's eyes blink.)

VOICE: *(O S)* There's nothing to fear now. I've got everything under control.

(The baby's eyes blink.)

VOICE: *(O S)* You're safe.

END OF PLAY